Contents

A musician's son

Galileo Galilei was born near Pisa, Italy in 1564. His father, Vincenzo, earned his living as a musician. He taught Galileo and his brother to play the lute. The Galilei family were not rich but they were not poor either.

Galileo's birthplace is famous for the Leaning Tower of Pisa, completed in 1372.

SCIENTISTS

GALILEO GALILEI

Sarah Ridley

W

FRANKLIN WATTS
LONDON•SYDNEY

Franklin Watts

Published in Great Britain in 2017 by
The Watts Publishing Group

Copyright © The Watts Publishing Group, 2014

All rights reserved.

Editor in chief: John C. Miles
Design: Jonathan Hair and Matt Lilly
Art director: Peter Scoulding
Picture research: Diana Morris
Original design concept: Sophie Williams

Picture credits: ESA/NASA: front cover b/g. Mary Evans PL: 22. Fine
Art Images/HIP/Topfoto: 19. Chris Go/Gemini Altair/NASA: front
cover tl. Istoria e Dimostrazioni,1613,Galileo: 14.JPL/DLR/NASA:
13. JPL/NASA: front cover tr. Luciano Mortula/Shutterstock: 4.
NASA: 23. Nimatallah/De Agostini/The Art Archive: 5.
Sage Ross/CC Wikimedia Commons: 9. © 2014 Photo Scala
Florence: 6–7. Science Museum/S&SPL: 21. Sidereus Nuncius/
University of Oklahoma Libraries: 11. SOHO/ESA/NASA: 15.
Wellcome Library, London: 17. CC Wikimedia Commons:
front cover c, 1, 8, 10, 12, 18, 20.

*Every attempt has been made to clear copyright. Should there be any
inadvertent omission please apply to the publisher for rectification.*

Dewey number: 520.9'2
ISBN: 978 1 4451 5358 2

Printed in China

Franklin Watts
An imprint of Hachette Children's Group
Part of The Watts Publishing Group
Carmelite House, 50 Victoria Embankment
London EC4Y 0DZ

An Hachette UK Company

www.hachette.co.uk
www.franklinwatts.co.uk

FSC
www.fsc.org
MIX
Paper from
responsible sources
FSC® C104740

1564–1573

An Italian lute player.

In Italy at that time, educated people were questioning old ideas about science and art in the face of new ones. This was called the Renaissance. Galileo's father experimented with the science of sound. He encouraged his son Galileo to question ideas and be curious.

1450–1750

The powerful local rulers, the Medici family, give support to thinkers and artists, making the Italian city of Florence a centre of new ideas.

1564

Galileo is born, the first of several children in the family.

1570s

He attends a local school.

His father is often working away from home, in the city of Florence 70 kilometres (43 miles) away.

Taught by monks

When he was ten, Galileo's family moved to Florence. His father arranged for Galileo to study at a local monastery famous for its clever monks. He learnt maths, religious studies, astrology and how to argue, write and draw well.

Galileo decided that he too would like to be a monk, but his father had other ideas. He wanted his son to be a doctor. He brought Galileo back home and then sent him to live with a relative in Pisa.

1574–1579

Galileo studied at the monastery at Vallombrosa, shown here in a 16th century painting.

1574

The family moves to Florence for the father's work.

1575–79

Galileo studies at the monastery at Vallombrosa.

1579

He returns to live with his family and then goes back to Pisa, to live with a relative.

He continues studying. He is bright enough to go to university but he's too young.

Medicine or maths?

At 16, Galileo started at university, studying to become a doctor. However, he eventually persuaded his father to let him change to maths. A few years later, he got a job as a professor, first at Pisa, and then at the University of Padua in northern Italy.

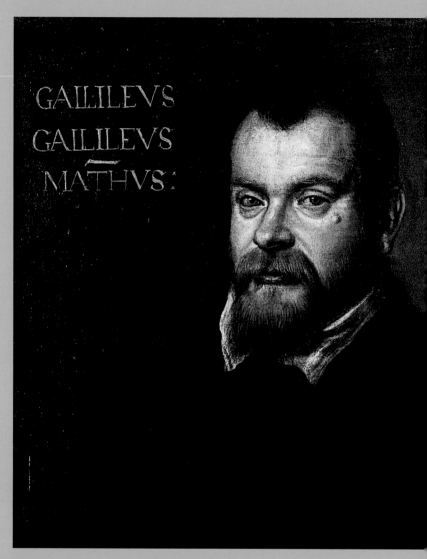

This portrait of Galileo was painted when he was a professor at Padua.

1580–85	**1585**	**1589**	**1591**
Galileo studies at the University of Pisa.	He leaves university without a degree and works as a teacher.	He becomes a professor at the University of Pisa.	His father dies.

1580–1608

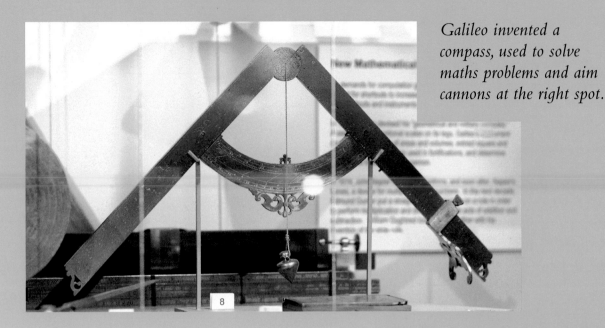

Galileo invented a compass, used to solve maths problems and aim cannons at the right spot.

Galileo was well paid and happy in his new job. He stayed in Padua for the next 18 years and started a family there. He was allowed plenty of time to develop his ideas. He experimented with how the speed of an object might change as it falls. Some of his ideas went against what was being taught in universities at that time.

BREAKTHROUGH

A story is told of how Galileo watched a huge lamp swing in the breeze in Pisa Cathedral, and how he timed it using his own pulse. He realised that a pendulum swings at a constant rate, and that it could be used to time things accurately.

1592

He becomes Chief Professor of Maths at the University of Padua.

1593–1606

He invents a pump, a geometric compass and a thermometer.

1599

He meets Marina di Andrea Gamba. They will have three children: Virginia, Livia and Vincenzo.

Looking at the Moon

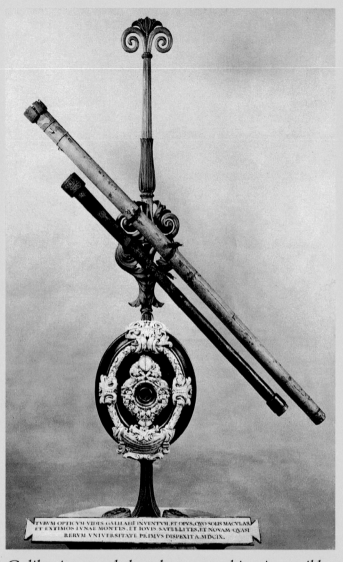

TVBVM OPTICVM VIDES GALILAEI INVENTVM ET OPVS, QVO SOLIS MACVLAS ET INTIMOS IVNAE MONTES, ET IOVIS SATELLITES, ET NOVAM QVASI RERVM VNIVERSITATE PRIMVS DISPEXIT A. MDCIX.

In May 1609 a friend wrote to Galileo describing a telescope. Without seeing one, Galileo built a better one. By the end of 1609 Galileo was spending a huge amount of time studying the night sky.

Galileo improved the telescope, making it possible to bring distant planets into view.

1608	**1609**	**1609–11**
Hans Lippershey, working in the Netherlands, invents the first telescope.	Galileo develops a telescope that is eight times, and eventually 30 times, more powerful than the first telescope.	Thomas Harriot in England uses a telescope to make maps of the Moon.

1609–1610

Galileo spotted mountains on the Moon, the millions of stars that make up the Milky Way and four of Jupiter's moons. He drew pictures of what he saw and included them in a book. His ideas and his book shot him to fame – and a new job.

Galileo's drawings of the Moon, showing its uneven surface.

EXPERIMENT

If you have a pair of binoculars at home, you too can see the Moon as Galileo did. Look at the Moon when it is a crescent or half moon as you will be able to see its craters and other features.

1609

Galileo makes detailed drawings of the Moon.

1610

He sees four moons around Jupiter and names them the Medicean Stars after Cosimo of Medici, the ruler of Florence.

1610

His book, *The Starry Messenger*, is published. He returns to Pisa to a top job at the university and at the court of the Medici family.

Copernicus and Galileo

1610

Galileo moves house, to live in the countryside outside Florence.

At this time, most people believed that the Earth was at the centre of the Universe and that the Sun went around the Earth, as described by the Greek thinker Aristotle. Galileo had long believed that it was in fact the Earth and the other planets that went around the Sun, following the ideas of astronomer Nicolaus Copernicus.

1611

He studies Saturn and Venus, noticing that Venus has phases and so is lit up by reflected light from the Sun.

1611

He travels to Rome to show his discoveries to important people in the Roman Catholic Church, including Pope Paul V. All goes well.

A painting of the Universe as Copernicus (1473–1543) saw it, with all the planets rotating around the Sun.

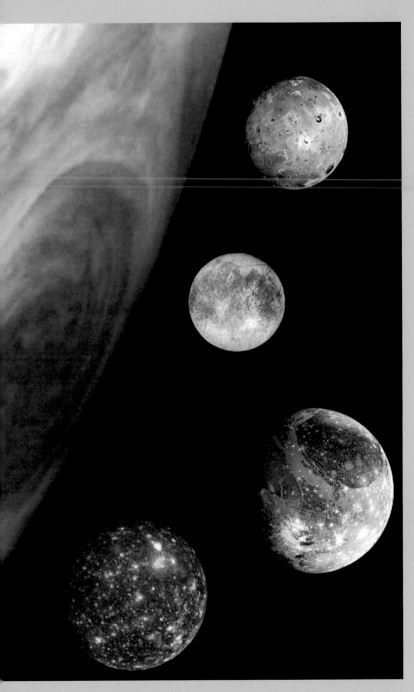

In his new job at Pisa, Galileo was free to follow his ideas. He continued to study and record the night sky, moving on from Jupiter to Saturn and Venus. All his work was proving one thing – all the planets, including the Earth, go around the Sun.

Jupiter and its four largest moons.

BREAKTHROUGH

When Galileo spotted four moons revolving around Jupiter, it proved that not everything revolved around the Earth. We now know that Jupiter has over 60 moons.

Star gazing

Now Galileo turned his attention, and his telescope, to the Sun. Over several weeks he drew and noted down sunspots. He watched them form, change and disappear on the surface of the Sun.

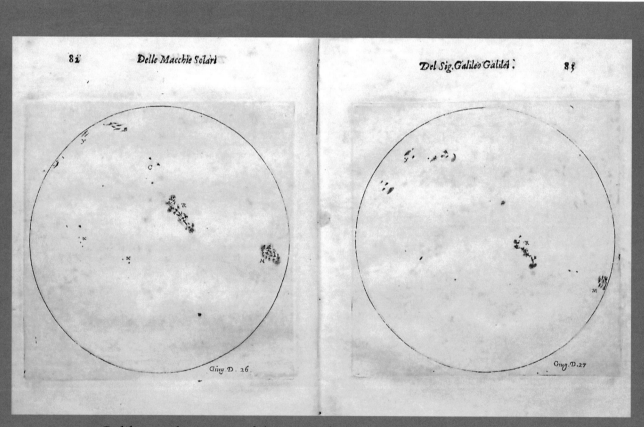

Galileo made a series of drawings showing sunspots on the Sun.

1611

Galileo publishes his ideas about how and why things float.

1611–13

He studies sunspots and draws them in notebooks. Looking directly at the Sun damaged Galileo's eyesight for good.

BREAKTHROUGH

Galileo's drawings of sunspots showed that the Sun was not a perfect ball of fire in the sky – it had sunspots. He also noticed that the position of the sunspots changed, day to day, proving that the Sun was spinning.

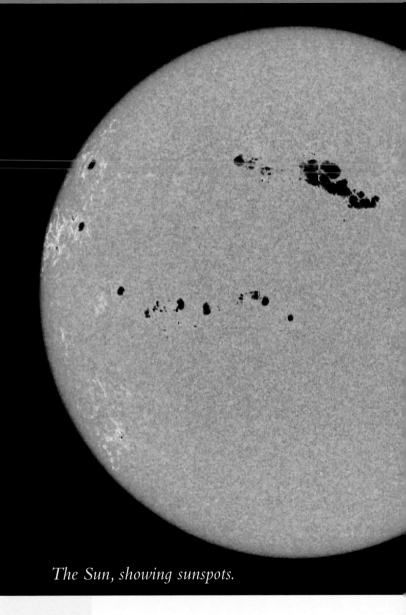

The Sun, showing sunspots.

Some important people in the Church found this idea very difficult to accept. They still believed Aristotle's idea that the Sun was a perfect ball of fire in the sky, never changing as it circled around the Earth.

1613

Galileo publishes a book about sunspots and sets out other ideas in writings at this time.

1613

Galileo arranges for his two daughters to live in a convent and become nuns.

Church trouble

The Roman Catholic Church held great power over everybody in Italy at this time. It dealt with ideas that it didn't like by bringing them before a Church court, called the Inquisition. It decided to investigate whether Galileo's ideas went against the teachings of the Church.

Here is part of a letter Galileo wrote in 1615, setting out his ideas:

I hold that the Sun is located at the centre of the revolutions of the heavenly orbs (planets) and does not change place, and that the Earth rotates on itself and moves around it.

1615	1616	1617
The Inquisition considers the new ideas about the Universe.	The Inquisition (and therefore the Church) forbids Galileo from teaching or publishing his ideas and bans several other books on the same subject.	Galileo moves house. He suffers from various illnesses.

A portrait of Galileo's eldest daughter Virginia, a nun. They wrote many letters to one another and Galileo often visited her.

In 1616 the Inquisition gave its verdict. They said that the idea that the Earth and the other planets went around the Sun was false. Galileo was warned not to teach or publish his views on this subject. He withdrew to a house in the countryside, close to the convent where his daughters lived, and carried on working.

1619/1623

He publishes his ideas on comets, which he thought were caused by a trick of light. He was wrong about this.

1624

Pope Urban VIII allows Galileo to write about his ideas but only as mathematical ideas.

1631

Galileo moves to a house closer to Arcetri, where his daughters live in a convent.

17

In great danger

For the next 15 years, Galileo continued to test out his ideas about maths and the Universe. In 1632 he published his ideas in a new book. In it he invented a character called Simplicio. Two other characters argue with him about science, explaining why it is true that the Earth and the other planets revolve around the Sun.

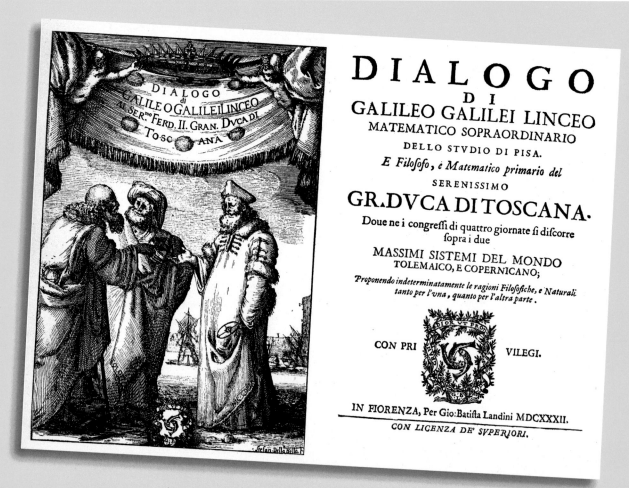

These pages from Galileo's book show Simplicio and the other characters arguing about science.

1632-33

Galileo had to defend his ideas before the Inquisition. It had the power to put him in prison, torture him or even put him to death.

The new book made Church leaders furious with Galileo and he was called to appear before the Inquisition. Old, ill and terrified of what might happen to him, Galileo travelled to Rome. He was questioned about his ideas – and was forced to deny his belief about the Earth turning around the Sun.

1632
Galileo publishes *Dialogue Concerning the Two Chief World Systems.*
Many scientists and astronomers read his book and are amazed.
He is ordered to appear before the Inquisition.

1633

Galileo travels to Rome and is kept as a prisoner. He appears before the Inquisition.

1633

He is forced to deny his idea that the Earth and other planets orbit around the Sun. He is sent to prison and his book is banned.

In prison at home

1634

Galileo's daughter, Virginia (Sister Maria Celeste), dies.

1638

He publishes his ideas about maths and the science of movement.

1638

Famous poet, John Milton, visits Galileo at home.

1641

Galileo describes the design for a pendulum clock that kept time much more accurately than clocks at that time.

Galileo was allowed to leave prison but he had to remain under house arrest, first in Rome and then back at home in Florence. His house was watched and only a few people were allowed to visit him.

This portrait of Galileo painted in 1640 shows him in old age, holding a telescope in his hand.

Galileo lived a lonely life in the countryside and was heartbroken when his eldest daughter, Virginia, died. He went blind and depended on his friends and students to write his ideas down. Still he carried on working, on maths and on the science of machines and movement.

After his father's death, Vincenzo Galileo and others built a pendulum clock similar to this one, using Galileo's ideas.

Galileo's ideas live on

Galileo died at home, aged 77.

In 1642 Galileo died, with his son and his students by his bedside. One of his students, Viviani, would go on to write down all he knew of Galileo and his ideas, providing an important record for historians.

1642	**1649**	**1642–1703**
Galileo dies.	Vincenzo, his son, builds a pendulum clock as described by his father.	Viviani keeps Galileo's notebooks and papers safe, working on the first biography of Galileo, eventually published years later in 1711.

1642–present day

Galileo helped us to look at the world in a new way. He tested out ideas, using maths and observations to prove them. Over 300 years later, an astronaut proved one of Galileo's ideas. He dropped a hammer and a feather on the Moon, where there is no gravity, to see whether they would fall at the same speed. And they did, as Galileo had predicted.

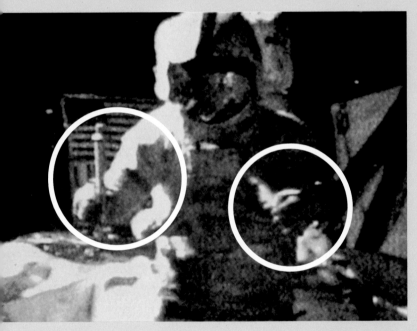

Astronaut, David Scott, drops a hammer and a feather (circled) on the Moon in 1971, proving Galileo's idea.

BREAKTHROUGH
Galileo tested out his ideas by carrying out experiments and tests. He kept detailed calculations to record what he observed. Scientists today still follow this way of investigating ideas.

1758
The Church lifts the ban on books that supported the idea that the planets revolve around the Sun.

1971
An astronaut performs the feather and the hammer experiment.

1992
Pope John Paul II admits Galileo was treated badly.

23

Glossary

Aristotle (394–322BCE) Greek philosopher whose ideas were still held to be true in Galileo's lifetime.

astrology The study of the stars in the sky and how they affect life on Earth.

astronomer An expert who studies stars, planets and outer space.

convent/nun A religious community where nuns live.

gravity A force of attraction between all objects.

house arrest A form of punishment when someone is not free to leave their home.

Inquisition The court set up in the 13th century by the Roman Catholic Church to investigate ideas that went against their teachings.

monastery/monk A religious community where monks live.

NASA The part of the US Government dedicated to their space program.

orb A round object.

pendulum A rod with a weighted end.

Pope/Roman Catholic Church The head of the Roman Catholic Church, a Christian Church based in Rome, Italy.

sphere A round, solid object.

sunspot A darker, cooler area on the Sun's surface.

Universe Everything that is known to exist – our galaxy and all the others.

To see the original television recording of the *Apollo 15* hammer and the feather experiment in 1971, go to: https://youtu.be/oYEgdZ3iEKA